Reporting the World

JOHN PILGER'S GREAT EYEWITNESS PHOTOGRAPHERS

This book is dedicated to the memory of Eric Piper, David Munro and Curt Gunther

First published worldwide in 2001 by 21 Publishing Ltd

Unit 204
Buspace Studios
Conlan Street
London W10 5AP

www.21publishing.com
tel: 020 8964 1113
fax: 020 8964 9993

ISBN 1 901785 09 2

Designed by Joe Ewart for Society
Edited by Miranda Glover, 21 Publishing Ltd
Production coordinated by Uwe Kraus
Printed in Italy

A catalogue record for this book is available from the British Library

In association with the exhibition
Reporting the World:
John Pilger's Great Eyewitness Photographers
26 July – 30 September 2001
Barbican Gallery, Barbican Centre
London EC2Y 8DS

Barbican Art Galleries are owned, funded and managed by the
Corporation of London

Cover Photograph
Robert Kennedy and John Pilger on a plane flying to Los Angeles,
Curt Gunther, June 1968

Exhibition Curator: Conrad Bodman
Exhibition Organiser: Alison Green
Curatorial Assistant: Sophie Persson

Also from 21 Publishing:

Blimey! From Bohemia to Britpop:
The London Artworld from Francis Bacon to Damien Hirst
Matthew Collings (photography: Ian MacMillan)
220 x 185mm   208pp   208 colour illustrations
ISBN 1 901785 00 9

Nat Tate
An American Artist: 1928–1960
William Boyd
210 x 160 mm   71pp   36 illustrations
ISBN 1 901785 01 7

It Hurts: New York Art from Warhol to Now
Matthew Collings (photography: Ian MacMillan)
220 x 185mm   232pp   208 colour illustrations
ISBN 1 901785 03 3

Peter Lanyon: At the edge of landscape
Chris Stephens
250 x 200mm   192pp   106 colour illustrations
ISBN 1 901785 04 1

William Tillyer: Against the Grain
Norbert Lynton
176pp   176 colour + 24 black and white illustrations
ISBN 1 901785 05 X

Bacon's Eye
Works on paper attributed to Francis Bacon from the Barry Joule
Archive
essay by Mark Sladen; interview with Barry Joule
in conjunction with the Barbican
112pp   116 colour illustrations
ISBN 1 901785 06 8

For further information about 21 Publishing,
visit our website at www.21publishing.com
or email us at info@21publishing.com

For stockist information, call 21 Publishing:
00 44 208 964 1113

Reporting the World

JOHN PILGER'S GREAT EYEWITNESS PHOTOGRAPHERS

THE PHOTOGRAPHERS

Keith Bernstein

Tom Buist

Steve Cox

Nic Dunlop

Gerrit Fokkema

John Garrett

Curt Gunther

Matt Herron

Philip Jones Griffiths

Marion Kaplan

Susan Meiselas

David Munro

John Pilger

Eric Piper

Ken Regan

Penny Tweedie

Anastasia Vrachnos

Paul Weinberg

CONTENTS

Introduction   6
By John Pilger

Cambodia
Eric Piper, John Pilger, Nic Dunlop   21

Burma
Nic Dunlop   28

Indonesia
Anastasia Vrachnos   32

Vietnam
David Munro, Philip Jones Griffiths   34

Philippines
David Munro   40

East Timor
Steve Cox   42

Bangladesh
Eric Piper, Penny Tweedie   47

USA
Matt Herron, Ken Regan, Curt Gunther   53

South Africa
Paul Weinberg, Keith Bernstein   72

Nicaragua
Susan Meiselas   76

Kenya
Marion Kaplan   80

Japan
Shigeru Oda   83

Australia
Penny Tweedie, Gerrit Fokkema   85

El Salvador
Eric Piper   94

United Kingdom
Tom Buist, John Garrett   96

Soviet Union
Eric Piper   110

Reporting the World

JOHN PILGER'S GREAT EYEWITNESS PHOTOGRAPHERS

This collection of photographs, selected from the Barbican exhibition, *Reporting the World*, is the realisation of a fond ambition of mine. Almost from the day I went on the road as a newspaper correspondent in the 1960s, I worked with photographers. We were a team, often assigned to places of upheaval, but also to peaceful streets, the sinews of people's lives, to ask ordinary people to tell their extraordinary stories in words and pictures. Time and curiosity were allowed then, and generous space on the page was devoted to worlds far removed from London's media village; and not because of the importance of the images in a current geo-political game. This was a new kind of reportage, pioneered in post-war Britain by *Picture Post*, following *Life* and *Look* magazines, whose essays allowed pictures and words to complement each other and the meaning of both to speak to the reader.

In bringing together this selection my aim has been to show how great photographers are both story-tellers and truth-tellers, going against the consensual versions of events, such as the illusions of 'booming' economies and 'smart' wars, and the judgement of humanity as worthy and unworthy, sacrosanct or expendable, by great power. This is not to suggest that a photograph 'says it all'. On the contrary, words are often vital to draw out the narrative and intrinsic

mysteries of documentary photographs. The two forms serve each other, and my best work, I believe, has been produced in harness, and comradeship, with some of the great photographers of my time. 'Much as I love reading words,' wrote Alberto Manuel in his appreciative *Reading Pictures*, 'I also love reading pictures, and I love reading the stories woven into them.' He meant also the stories about their creators. He called 'witness' photography the 20th century's 'emblematic art form'.

I agree wholeheartedly. This book and the associated exhibition are my personal tribute to photographers with whom I have worked as a writer during more than three decades. Most of these pictures were taken on shared assignments. Certainly, there is nostalgia in my wanting to show off their work; but the edge to this display is not about looking back: it is about looking forward, and calling on those who value photo-journalism to break the silence on what has been done to a craft now relegated, more often than not, to the service of 'infotainment' and other anti-journalism. Consider this irony. As media technology has advanced and become 'global', so journalism, especially photo-journalism, has become increasingly parochial, prurient and politically safe. The great documentary form, the still photograph, has become largely a fashion and fame vehicle, answering to the incessant demands of the 'market', serving what *Time* magazine calls 'the eternal present'. As for people's true lives, these are deemed unprofitable and of minimal interest.

There remain outstanding exceptions to this. By honouring the work of some of them, I hope this book and The Barbican exhibition will be a rallying cry for the renewal of photo-journalism as the first draft of people's history that journalism ought to be. For example, in 1972, I went to Murton, a colliery village in County Durham with the photographer Tom Buist, beginning a relationship with a community whose struggle Tom and later John Garrett recorded in superb documentary photographs, published in *The Daily Mirror* and *The Guardian* respectively. There is the haunting image of Joe Cardy, framed in the half-light on the pithead at the end of his shift. He is exhausted, having worked a deep seam below the North Sea, bringing up props like an artilleryman under fire, in a tunnel barely four feet high and often awash. And there he is again, home and scrubbed and with a laconic smile, holding up his payslip with its miserly sum. Following the Great Strike of 1984/5, Murton was the last pit to return to work. Through that morning's mist, they marched back behind the brass band, with the women leading: for me, Britain at its best. Six years later, with the pit long closed and Joe Cardy worked literally to death, I returned with John Garrett, whose photographs evoke George Orwell's *The Road to Wigan Pier*. On the long, black beach at Easington we found redundant men, picking coal, while their wives and girlfriends, mothers and sisters, tended a picket line at the one remaining

mine. A decade on, it is 2001, and John's portrait of the north of England is without a trace of the pits, as if they never existed. They are pictures of a quiet desolation, of 'flexible working' and a poverty unseen.

Nic Dunlop's work in south east Asia deserves the recognition given to veterans who may be better known. Nic has been a pioneer in documenting, in Cambodia, the devastation wrought by landmines, a worldwide plague. He has exposed the illegitimate Burmese regime's slave labour, and illuminated the heroism of Aung San Suu Kyi and her pro-democracy comrades. Single-handed, he tracked down one of the most infamous and elusive of the Khmer Rouge leaders, Kaing Khek Iev, alias 'Deuch', who ran Cambodia's Tuol Sleng Prison, where more than 20,000 people were tortured and killed. Having carried a photo of Deuch in his backpocket, Nic spotted him wearing an American Refugee Committee T-shirt. 'I am now a Christian,' he told Nic. He is now awaiting trial in Phnom Penh, having confirmed to Nic that the Khmer Rouge had deliberately planned mass murder. It was a brilliant scoop. Yet apart from the *Far Eastern Economic Review*, newspapers and magazines showed little interest or rejected his story and pictures outright. The Khmer Rouge were no longer 'news fashionable'. What this suggests is that photo-journalism has come under such pressure, much of it devalued and trivialised, that the craft judgement of some editors, their 'news sense', has been lost, or has succumbed to the blight of giving-the-public-what-they-want: code for giving the public no choice. Nic's tenacity is more than matched by his compassion; watching him work with ordinary people, I am touched always by his respect for them: his gentle, rather bashful inquisitiveness that permits them to trust him. In 1995, he and I went back to the Vietnamese village of My Lai, where the famous massacre took place in 1968. His pictures recalled its survivors and their memories in such a way that, when they were published by *The Guardian* magazine, the horror at last seemed human.

Like Nic Dunlop, Steve Cox is a self-effacing man, belying a burning passion for his craft. Recently, Steve took a staff job on *The Glasgow Sunday Herald* which, by going against the trend and displaying fine black-and-white pictures uncropped and across most of a page, has become, pictorially, one of the most attractive newspapers in Britain today. For most of his career, Steve, like Nic and so many other photographers, has struggled to make a living. Self-taught, he began his photographic career in advertising, where the ethos was not what he had in mind. 'I found on a trip to the Middle East,' he said, 'that my affinity was with indigenous peoples; I wanted to show the injustices done to them.' He decided to fund himself, 'to live off my wits' and in the 1980s, he reached the destroyed town of Halabja in Iraq, where Saddam Hussein had used gas against the Kurdish population, killing 5,000 people. His photographs appeared in *The Independent*. In 1991, again, without funding, he set out for East Timor, where, according to Amnesty International, a third of the population, more than 200,000 people, had perished under the Indonesian occupation. Published in *Newsweek* and elsewhere, his photographs of life and death in a country whose suffering was effectively a secret, are unique in their portrayal of the everyday banalities and subtleties of oppression. There is the Indonesian soldier examining a ceremonial sword, a family keepsake, which he has just wrested from a Timorese man. The soldier is clearly pondering whether to steal it, and the nervous smiles of the man and his family are of people powerless before arbitrary power. It is an image of colonialism.

It was Steve Cox's photographs of a massacre of unarmed students in the Santa Cruz cemetery in the East Timorese capital, Dili, that helped alert the world to the genocide. Steve had followed a procession of young people into the graveyard for the funeral of a student shot by the Indonesians. He was in the small chapel when soldiers attacked them, shooting at point blank range. 'I expected not to come out of there alive,' he told me. 'Bullets were hitting the walls and coming through the windows. The wounded had struggled or had been dragged there, and I felt that all I could do, in these last moments, was to record the crime. I was taking pictures when two soldiers burst in and dragged me along a dirt track, kicking and rifle-butting me. I could see heaps of corpses being loaded on to a military truck. I was thrown down and a gun was put to my temple and a bayonet to my throat. It was then that a plain-clothed officer intervened and had me thrown into another truck. I was taken to a police station and with Chris Wenner [the British cameraman whose videotape of the massacre was shown around the world] I was eventually let go. Incredibly, my camera bag stayed over my shoulder and no one bothered to take my film.' When he flew to Australia from West Timor, Steve was the only passenger to be body-searched by Australian officials, whose government recognised General Suharto's illegal occupation. 'It was clear they had been tipped off by the Indonesians and were looking for the film,' he said, 'They were disappointed because I had given it to another passenger, who hid it and got it through the airport for me.'

As a member of the public, says Steve, 'I believe we don't have the right to be shielded from the hell that other people are suffering. If people in this country don't like it, they shouldn't buy a Sunday paper. But it's significant that since lifestyle journalism took over and the bottom has dropped out of photo-journalism, sales of Sunday newspapers have fallen. I believe people want to know, and are prepared to be disturbed, so that they can understand something of why great injustice happens.'

Not long ago, the American photographer Ken Jarecke was talking about censorship by omission as the most virulent form of censorship in the 'free' press. His was the breath-catching picture of an Iraqi burnt to a blackened cinder, petrified at the wheel of his vehicle on the Basra Road where, along with hundreds of others, he was massacred by American pilots on their infamous 'turkey shoot' at the end of the 1991 Gulf war. *The Observer* published the picture, though not on the front page, where it belonged. In the United States, it was suppressed until long after the war was over, because this single image stripped away the propaganda that war had at last become a bloodless science: 'clean' and 'surgical'. 'No one would touch my photograph,' he said. 'The excuse was that it was too upsetting: that people don't want to look at that kind of thing any more. The truth was that the whole US press collaborated in keeping silent about the consequences of the Gulf war and who was responsible.'

His words have a timeless quality. For me, they recall *The War Primer*, which the playwright and poet Bertolt Brecht put together while he was a refugee from Nazi Germany. With a four-line poem beneath a war photograph on each page, Brecht shifted horror and pity to anger and responsibility. Under a picture of a mother looking for her family in a bombed-out house, he wrote:

> Stop searching, woman: you
> will never find them
> But, woman, don't accept that
> Fate is to blame.
> Those murky forces, woman,
> that torment you
> Have each of them a face,
> address and name.

Many of the photographs in these pages honour the tradition Brecht describes: of ideas and images that both shock and make people think more deeply about reasons why. To those who would draw a veil over great crimes, Ken Jarecke and Steve Cox are dangerous men. So, too, is the Magnum photographer Philip Jones Griffiths, with whom I worked in Vietnam at the height of that war. The subversive quality of Philip's pictures is, in my view, without equal. Combined with a humanity that is a presence in all his work, the power of his pictures always stirs me, as if he has pushed back a screen and said, 'Here, this is what you should see and know.' To understand what really happened in Vietnam, and why, one need look no farther than *Vietnam Inc.*, Philip's classic work, which is not strictly a picture book; his words are as fine. Beneath a Goya-like picture of a captured Vietcong soldier, prostrate and surrounded in the darkness, he wrote: 'It is difficult to avoid the conclusion that the effect of American involvement in Vietnam has been to differentiate the most admirable Vietnamese from the most deplorable. The values that the Vietnamese regard highly are possessed almost exclusively by the Vietcong.' These values, he pointed out, are nowhere better set down in writing than in the national poem *Kim Van Kieu*, which is a veritable handbook on the Vietnamese psyche, yet is virtually unread by Americans. In it is chronicled the life of the heroine, Thuy Kieu, with whom the Vietnamese, as a nation, identify [and who] declared in the poem:

> *It is better that I should sacrifice myself alone*
> *It matters little if a flower falls if the tree can*
> *keep its leaves green ...*

His image of two GIs with a Vietnamese woman, a paid-for rape, is the war's degradation. His spruce American war planners in their operations bubble in Saigon, transfixed by IBM computer print-outs, are its madness. His caption, reflecting his mischievous, dry humour, reads: '[This] is the computer that proves the war is being won. Data collected for the Hamlet Evaluation System is analysed by it to see who loves us. Optimistic results on the my-wife-is-not-trying-to-poison-me-therefore-she-loves-me pattern are reliably produced, each and every month.' These absurd figures appear in much of Philip's work, the embodiment of military idiocy and incompetence. They are Yossarin and Major Major from the great American anti-war novel, *Catch-22*. Indeed, Philip may well be photo-journalism's Joseph Heller, a master of black irony.

In 1970, at the end of our first assignment in Saigon, Philip handed me, not a bundle of rolls of film, not copious sheets of contact prints over which my picture editor in London would pore, but a used brown envelope containing six photographs. He watched, straight-faced, eyes twinkling, enjoying my reaction. I was aghast – until I looked. Each print was exquisite in its symbolism and true to everything we had seen in Vietnam and talked about, especially the destructive relationship between the Vietnamese and the Americans. One picture was of a large GI in a crowd of busy, opaque Vietnamese faces that included a young woman photographed in the act of picking his pocket, and picking it elegantly, so that her little finger extended. Philip had waited days on the balcony of the Royale Hotel for this picture, his war-weary Leica expending less than a single roll of film. Just as his rape picture was the American invasion, so this was the invaders' vulnerability and their coming defeat.

Gerrit Fokkema's pictures of Australia's hidden poor are also both subversive and humane. The old man in a western Sydney trailer park, sitting in his minute garden, is respected by the photographer, yet his poverty marks his distance from Australia's clichéd image of sunny prosperity. As revealing is a portrait of two Australian Vietnam veterans, bedecked in medals and flags, belying the truth that both men are terribly disabled: until you study them and see the pain and anger caught in their eyes. Brian Day, who suffers from the effects of the herbicide spray, 'Agent Orange', used by the Americans to defoliate Vietnam's forests, described the war as 'a criminal act'. He told me, 'I remember one night a senior American officer said he had nothing but praise for the expertise and discipline of the Australian soldier. He said, "We really like having you guys here; you've helped us a lot. It's like the British having the Gurkhas, we have the Australians."'

In 1987, Gerrit Fokkema and I gained access to the Maralinga nuclear test site in the central Australian desert, where the British exploded their atomic bombs on Aboriginal land in the 1950s. For me, the most telling image is that of a lavatory bowl on its concrete mount in the desert, a solitary monument to the scientists who came and contaminated an area the size of England.

The Aboriginal struggle has been a constant theme in my work, and one of its most incisive eyewitnesses is Penny Tweedie. Penny's photographs have appeared in several of the documentary films I have made with fellow Australian Alan Lowery. In 1975, an Aboriginal elder showed Penny secret marking and painting in caves near Alice Springs. He said to her, 'Take a picture of this, tell your people 'bout us, 'bout our land, our dreaming. Maybe they can understand, stop hurting us.' Penny has since worked to tell the outside world about the oldest continuous people on earth, who are still denied basic human rights. She remembers an American magazine turning down her pictures with a telex message dismissing the Aborigines as 'a depraved and deprived race'. Consider that sentiment, still commonly expressed in white Australia, against her picture of a black family, dignified, proud and hurt, with their bush home behind them, and of the angry politicised demonstrator, not untypical of many young urban Aborigines. No other photographer I know has

developed such a mutual trust with indigenous Australians. She told me how her son Ben, then a two-year-old, fell ill with a severe fever in remote country and how a medicine man called Milpurrurru 'dragged the fever out of him until Ben jumped up, as if nothing had happened.'

I first met Penny in 1971 in Bangladesh, where we were covering the war that brought independence to what had been East Pakistan. One episode produced a series of pictures that raised searching questions about the moral dilemmas and responsibilities of eyewitness photographers and continues to generate debate. The Bengali liberation militia, known as the Mukti Bahini, staged a victory rally in Dacca stadium before a crowd of 40,000. The world's press was there, and many of the journalists and photographers were frustrated that they had not seen much action in the war. Behind the speakers' podium, Penny found five young men tied together, guarded by militiamen. 'As I raised my camera,' she recalled, 'a guard lunged at one of his prisoners with a rifle butt. When I asked what was going on, he said nothing. The prisoners were really only boys. One of them pleaded to me, "Help us". Suddenly, they were dragged to their feet and marched into the stadium. When the crowd caught sight of them, people stood up and began singing prayers with their hands close to their faces. Some were crying. The prisoners were thrown to the ground, and the Mukti Bahini swarmed in and began to bash them. There were about a dozen foreign photographers, all snapping away and no one was trying to stop it. As soon as the Bengali leader, Saddiqui, a flamboyant character, arrived in the stadium, I had a very bad feeling that this torture was being staged for us, the media. The boy at my feet was looking desperately at me, terrified; behind him I saw one of the militia brandishing a bayonet. I turned to [the photographer] Mark Riboud and said, 'This is being done for us. We've got to stop it.' He felt the same: so did Richard Linley from ITN, and we walked away. Linley protested openly and tried to speak to Saddiqui, but got no sense out of him. The three of us called to the other photographers to back off, and we tried to set an example by walking towards the stadium gate. We later returned to find four of the boys dead on the ground. Someone said they had been collaborators. When I got back to the hotel, several photographers who had missed the killings wanted me to let them have my film, then accused me of being a coward: of failing in my duty as a correspondent. Months later, one of the photographers who stayed in the stadium won the Pulitzer Prize for his picture of a boy dying at the end of a bayonet.'

A few weeks earlier, something similar had happened to John Garrett and Eric Piper, who were with me for *The Daily Mirror*. We had reached the town of Jessore with a column of the Indian army, and a group of alleged collaborators were paraded before us. As John and Eric raised their cameras, the men were beaten with bamboo poles. The moment they stopped photographing and walked away, the beating stopped. No photography prize was won that day.

I have been fortunate to work on many assignments with two celebrated American photographers, Matt Herron and Ken Regan. As characters, they are very different: Matt, a Princeton graduate, is an intense mixture of professional photographer, writer and

activist; he was a conscientious objector during the Korean war. Ken is self-made to a tee; having grown up in Brooklyn's Irish and Italian quarter, he founded Camera 5, the New York agency whose photography epitomised the vibrancy of 1960s America; most of it was Ken's.

Matt's picture essays in *Life*, *Look* and the *Saturday Evening Post* are a distinguished chronicle of the civil rights struggle of the 1960s. At the start of the decade, he and his wife Jeannine were among the first 'freedom riders' to go to Mississippi. Matt set up the *Southern Documentary Project*, which encouraged young black (and white) photographers to record their changing, often violent environment. In 1968, I went to live in the United States and renewed my friendship with Matt; we had travelled through South America together on an assignment two years earlier. In the late 1960s, social and political revolutionaries were bursting from the margins of American society: those described by Martha Gellhorn as 'that life-saving minority of Americans … the people with a wakeful conscience.' We joined many of them on the Poor People's March from Atlanta, Georgia, which Martin Luther King was meant to lead; a month earlier he had been assassinated. I can still hear *We Shall Overcome* hummed by the marchers as we passed through hostile white 'Dixie'. Matt's almost forensic, yet profoundly stirring pictures of the faces of both the oppressed and their oppressors ran across the centre pages of *The Daily Mirror*, beneath the headline: 'To be poor in America is to be un-American'. Such was the quality of the western world's biggest selling tabloid in the years before Murdoch transformed journalism in Britain.

Two years later, in an Ohio town called Beallsville, where it was heresy to question duty to God and country, we found patriotism itself challenged by the suspicion that people's sons had gone to Vietnam and died in the cause of nothing. 'I thought it was somewhere near Panama: real close and threatening,' recalled Maegene Pittman, whose son Jack had been killed. The national ratio for Americans killed in Vietnam was one in 6,000; for Beallsville it was one in 90. This was the town that lost the war. The graves of its sons cluttered the hillside overlooking the high school they had attended. Matt's portrait of the town and especially of the parents are searing. There is Betty and Kenneth Rucker, holding the decorations awarded to their son, Rick, standing outside their small home, their hurt consuming all; they had refused a military funeral. Ten years later, I returned to Beallsville to find that all the parents we'd met had gone. Some had moved away; most had died.

When Ken Regan and I went to Detroit in the early 1970s, every major corporation was laying off men, and there was great anger in a city that was the harbinger of the dream of full, secure employment. Ken's pictures of those who had never known unemployment, such as members of the United Auto Workers' Union, say much about working Americans who never believed this could happen to them. Detroit then had the most intractable poverty in America, and at a soup kitchen the anger engulfed us. We ran to our car, only to find that I had locked the keys inside. So we kept on running. An occupational hazard, it was one of a number of athletic feats performed in the company of Regan and Herron. In Montgomery, Alabama, Matt and I were obliged to run from a

cinema, where we had gone to see the John Wayne movie *The Green Berets*, unwisely, on a Saturday night. Unable to restrain my reaction to Wayne's fake heroism in a mythical Vietnam, my laughter so inflamed the audience of white 'good old boys' that Matt, sensing danger, said, 'Let's *get*!'

Having grown up in New York's gangland, Ken had antennae for violence. In Hunts Point in the South Bronx, then the most violent square mile in the western world, we spent several days and nights with two cops from a precinct so besieged that 'Do Not Cross' barriers were placed *inside* the police station. It was known as *Fort Apache*; and the bulletin board carried this sign: 'Assume that all combatants use high power military-type weapons for sniping and Molotov cocktails for ambushing'. As we ran with the cops pursuing ubiquitous 'suspects' down alleys, up stairwells and across rooftops, their guns permanently drawn, it was difficult to tell who was chasing whom. When a woman knocked on the window of the patrol car and lunged at us with a foot-long knife, one of the cops twisted her wrist until she let it go. 'Hey, get out of here,' he said casually, 'You're always doing that to us.'

Ken's pictures are never of stereotypes. Like Tom Buist's portrait of Joe Cardy, he portrayed the cops as exhausted, often frightened. In the boot of their patrol car, patrolman Ken Kurtz kept children's shoes: the previous Christmas he had found two brothers, aged five and six, crying with frostbite. He talked incessantly about poverty being at the root of all the violence.'

Not quite all of it. The following year, Ken set up a

meeting with Joe Colombo, the famous Mafia boss on whom the Marlon Brando character in the movie *The Godfather* was based.

'Mr. Colombo, I asked him, how do you manage to spend 100,000 dollars a day if, as you say, you get only 20,000 from selling real estate?'
'Who put out that figure, 100,000?'
'The New York District Attorney.'
'How can he say that? That's inferring I'm dishonest. The poor guy obviously had no mother, or he's not Italian. Very, very sad guy.'
Two weeks later, Joe Colombo was shot on the pavement in Columbus Circle. He remained in a vegetative state for two years, surrounded by heart-shaped bouquets of flowers, then he died. Hollywood never matched Ken Regan's portraits of the authentic article.

Like his work in the South Bronx, Ken's pictures of the Guardian Angels, the self-appointed vigilantes of the New York subway, with whom we spent other sleepless nights, capture that vanishing point at the edge of American life where reality and fiction merge. Were these real characters? Yes, and no. One of my favourite Ken Regan pictures is of George Wallace, the governor of Alabama, seated beside Edward Kennedy, scion of Yankee liberalism. When he was thinking of running for president, the last of the Kennedy brothers flew down to Alabama to court Wallace, the old racist who claimed the power of 'delivering' the southern vote. The portrait of the two of them on a podium together, wincing or smiling, surrounded by 'good old boys', is a the epitome of ambition and opportunism, blissfully united.

Ken started Camera 5 with a photographer called Curt Gunther, with whom I often worked until his death in 1991. Only one photograph of Curt's appears in these pages, because all the others are missing, or they are in a garage in Nevada: no one is sure. This is a tragedy, though not surprising, because Curt's life seemed to beckon uncertainty, at times havoc. Born and brought up in Berlin, Curt acquired his first Leica camera at the age of thirteen, and photography became his obsession. His photographs of Berlin under the Nazis were first seen through the eyes of someone watching the approach of his own violent death. Curt was Jewish. During a parade of Nazi stormtroopers he was thrown into a doorway and arrested. He struggled free and eventually escaped abroad; his family perished in the death camps. When he arrived in New York, he was eighteen, broke and spoke no English. Remaining broke all his life, Curt bore a melancholia and chutzpah, an audacity and black humour, that distinguished many of his generation of German Jewish refugees. Above all, he loved to photograph boxing. Straight off the ship in 1938, he headed for Joe Louis' training camp in upstate New York where the world heavyweight champion was preparing to defend his title. Slipping past the guards, he managed to confront Louis and, with no English, asked if he could take his picture. Taken aback by this unusual person, Louis not only agreed, but handed Curt $100. *Life* magazine published the pictures, which are now photographic icons. Being Curt, disaster beckoned. Hitch-hiking back to the Louis camp, he fell asleep and found himself in Canada from where he was deported back to Germany. He escaped again, and returned to America.

Curt and I did many assignments together. We

investigated the environmental effects of nuclear testing in Nevada. On the way, we attended an Elvis Presley concert in Las Vegas where Elvis and Curt (in the front row, his bloodhound expression unchanged, his lips barely moving) sang a duet of *Blue Suede Shoes*. We later traced the epic journey in John Steinbeck's *Grapes of Wrath*; Curt's pictures of poor whites, once again on the move, were of another America, its cast-offs engraved against sweeping grey skies. The one photograph of Curt's I have is from June 1968. We were with Robert Kennedy on his campaign plane as he flew to Los Angeles. I had arranged an interview with Kennedy, who for some reason stipulated no pictures. As the candidate and I talked, there was a piercing 'Owww!'

A bony hand extending from the lavatory had been snapping Kennedy's picture when someone slammed the door on it. The same extraterrestrial periscope with a camera perched on the end then appeared next to our row of seats.

'What's this?' asked Kennedy.

'Curt Gunther', I said.

A face that tried to see through usually shattered pebble glasses, a face that never smiled, appeared at Kennedy's elbow. 'How do you do?' said Curt, as always overdoing the formality. He then took perhaps the finest, final pictures of the man who almost certainly would have been president and who, the next day, was fatally shot in the Ambassador Hotel, in front of me. The surviving picture is on the cover of this book.

The courage implicit in the working lives of great photographers is sometimes confused with the nihilistic bravado for which some of their war-chasing colleagues are famous. You would never know from their almost diffident way that Philip Jones Griffiths and Steve Cox had beckoned danger with their lens. This is also true of Susan Meiselas, like Philip a celebrated Magnum photographer, with whom I worked in Nicaragua. Susan documented the popular uprising, led by the Sandinistas, that overthrew the Somoza tyranny in 1979. She photographed frequently under fire, yet in her pictures there is an understanding of the endurance of civilians, even gentleness in her images of violence. Her picture of two children lying dying, having been rescued from their bombed home, is grievous, yet you do not look away; you ask *why*? There is her picture of the Pope, who had come to Nicaragua specifically to reclaim the Catholic Church from a priesthood whose 'liberation theology' had helped get rid of Somoza and who enjoyed immense popularity among the poor. Admonishing the priests before a vast crowd in Managua, His Holiness appears unaware that he is overshadowed by a huge, heroic image of Sandino, the revolution's icon. In Susan's picture, the hunched white figure looks powerless, almost irrelevant.

In 1968, I was in Kenya when the government in Nairobi raised the issue of residents without citizenship, causing great fear among Asians, most of whom held British passports. In London, racist immigration laws were hurriedly enacted by the Wilson Labour government, preventing these British passport holders from entering Britain. The issue was race; this was the year of Enoch Powell's Rivers of Blood speech. Thousands of Asians were stranded in East Africa, unable to apply for permits to work because they were citizens of another country – Britain. They began to starve, and were terrified –

with good cause, as Idi Amin later demonstrated in Uganda. Marion Kaplan and I listened to their stories. Marion was a chronicler of Africa, the first woman to sail as crew and as a photographer in a dhow on the ancient route from east Africa to the Persian Gulf. Her portraits of frightened people that were published with my reports are remarkable for both the desperation and dignity they convey. There was Chanchalgar Gosi, sitting bolt upright in the gutter. He had owned a shop and now used the pavement as a desk, writing letter upon letter to the British High Commission, the Queen, Harold Wilson. He showed us his diary. The last entry read: 'Pandit gave me two shillings in the most kind way. So today I shall eat.'

Like many foreign journalists whose work proved unpalatable to the apartheid regime, I was banned from South Africa after reporting from there in the 1960s. I have included here the work of Paul Weinberg, one of an outstanding group of South African photographers whose work was a beacon during the apartheid years. Although he and I could never work together, his pictures later became an important component of a documentary film I made when I was finally allowed back in 1997. That aside, I simply want to celebrate a unique branch of photo-journalism that became the 'eyes' of millions of people denied almost every human right.

There is Paul's historic image, so thrilling to behold, of a lone woman standing between two armoured military vehicles, known as 'hippos', as they rolled into her township. Her arms are raised, fists clenched. Paul's picture from May Day, 1985 is as fine. A woman taking part in a strike of a million and a half workers is confronted by the barrel of a police gun. She appears defiant, holding her ground, whereas the bearer of the gun seems unsure, perhaps even afraid. In the early 1980s, Paul was one of the founders of Afrapix, his country's first non-racial photographers' collective. Theirs was dangerous work. He wrote at the time, 'Journalists and photographers who now criticise the government or merely cover anti-apartheid events are seen to be 'media terrorists' who are part of the conspiracy theory that all that is opposition emanates from Moscow, even when it is on your front door.' These days, Paul prefers to play down 'marketing hero status', as he puts it, partly because he objects to what he calls the celebration of the 'phony concept' of 'a rainbow nation ... that vibrates with positivism'. My film, which featured his work, was entitled *Apartheid Did Not Die* and described the economic divisions that have deepened since liberation. 'Beyond the stereotypes that the world began to know as the truth,' he told me, 'are the gaps and cracks that reveal themselves: the ordinary people who in their way struggle to overcome and realise their dreams. In the gaps and the cracks is where I like to work.' He has since published books about indigenous peoples and rural communities that are eloquent, uncompromising testaments to understanding different lives, and therefore humanity itself. On my eventual return to South Africa, Paul gave me a gift of a photograph, which I prize. It is of people dancing for joy at the return of their ancestral land in the days following the first democratic elections in 1994. It expresses the optimistic, generous spirit of those who were not crushed, and it belongs beside his images from a resistance whose heroism I have no doubt he shares.

The work of John Garrett has a special place in these

pages. I have known and worked with John the longest of any photographer, over 30 years; we landed in London from Australia within a year or two of each other, and stayed. We both have an outsider's affection for this country, although at heart I suspect we are displaced persons. What always impresses me about John's photography is the wisdom of its observation. Although John's work is truly international, I cannot think of another photographer who has captured the often unseen side of Britain as he has. In 1970, John and I went on the road with Enoch Powell. This politician was fascinating; dressed in a black overcoat and black homberg, he saw himself as a Churchillian figure, awaiting the call to save the nation. Since his death, Powell has been paid copious respect for his intellect and oratory. In truth, he was a crude racist. With his supercilious whine, he delighted in humiliating Asian members of his audience who dared to challenge his bigotry, usually politely; and he conducted, like a maestro demagogue, the baying of his supporters. John's portraits of him and his people not only capture this truth, but invite us to reflect on the disguised, genteel face of fascism in Britain.

John's enduring achievement has been to peel away the masks of poverty in a developed society. No matter the fake designer jeans and trainers on the children in a Liverpool mall, no matter their defiant expressions, the images are of children whose future has been all but decided. Behind the jumping toddler are boarded windows; the Cut Price Mini Market is framed in razor wire; Front Street exists, with no humanity, like the vast empty Courtaulds factory in Nottingham, closed down by a man who has 're-structured' fifteen such factories and was himself made redundant. Most

modern poverty is internalised, rather than displayed, and that has not changed since John and I went to Liverpool in the 1970s. I made a film there about child poverty, called *Smashing Kids*, and John's black and white portraits were so incisive, yet respectful, that most of the film was given over to them. Technically, he has few equals in black and white photography, even though, oddly, he has trouble with machines. Testament to this are the 2,500,000 sales of his *The 35mm Photographers' Handbook*, published in 1979 and still in print throughout the world. Suffice to say that those who might doubt documentary photography's claim to be an art form need only look at the extraordinary range of John Garrett's work.

Eric Piper and I were a partnership on *The Daily Mirror* during the 1960s and 1970s when Hugh Cudlipp, the editor-in-chief, opened a map of the world before its millions of readers. This was Cudlipp's 'great adventure' and the result was the first truly internationalist tabloid newspaper. The brilliance of its editors and designers, Cudlipp himself, Tony Miles, Mike Molloy and Paddy O'Gara and many others, produced pages that allowed words and pictures a freedom hitherto, and since, almost unknown in the popular press.

Eric Piper, horn-rimmed glasses, balding and often chuckling, a photographer who never, to my knowledge, owned a camera bag (he preferred plastic airline bags, claiming they 'disguised' him) was the quintessential Fleet Street professional. He also loved cricket and sunshine. The nod-and-wink deal he had with *The Mirror* was that he would cover the MCC tour of the Caribbean, the Indian sub-continent or

Australia during the English winter, then join me in a place of similar clime. If the cricket was uninspiring, he would transfer to a royal tour, preferably of the South Pacific. Among his achievements was persuading Princess Anne to transform her expression of totemic disdain into a human smile. 'Is this all right, Mr. Piper?' she would warble.

Our first assignment together was an extended route march through the jungle of east Bengal, behind a green and red Bangladeshi flag and a ragged file of guerrillas armed with Lee Enfield rifles, several dating back to the First World War. We came upon villages razed by the Pakistani army, their occupants killed in what appeared to be a systematic slaughter of civilians. Eric's pictures provided some of the first evidence that the government in Islamabad was practising genocide in its eastern province. That was, I suppose, a precursor for many of our assignments that witnessed the struggle of people against colonial power. The only time he told me he wished he was back in a pavilion, hearing the crack of a small red ball on willow, was when we spent several months getting lost between Sudan and Eritrea; relentless sandstorms test the most stoic. We also worked in Central America, mostly El Salvador; and we travelled extensively in Vietnam during that country's imposed isolation following the war. On one of several assignments in the Soviet Union, Eric's latest airline bag was wrenched from his shoulder by two KGB goons, who had followed us to the Moscow home of the dissidents Vladimir and Maria Slepak. 'Pipes' duly wrenched it back, kicking one of the goons in the shin. He later claimed inspiration for this uncharacteristic show of force from nights out with the erstwhile England all-

rounder Ian Botham, his old pal. He loved children and he and his wife Beryl helped bring up several children from a disadvantaged home. For a single picture, only Eric could assemble hundreds, thousands if necessary, of kids and lead them, pied piper-like. I never saw him take a photograph of an impoverished and stricken child and not try to help; that is not always the case. His *Mirror* front page picture of the starving children of Biafra, the secessionist nation subjected to an embargo by the West, stirred the world and saved countless lives.

In the summer of 1979, Eric and I, with film director David Munro, cameraman Gerry Pinches and sound recordist Steve Phillips, went to Cambodia in the wake of the Vietnamese overthrow of Pol Pot and the genocidal Khmer Rouge. In Phnom Penh we encountered a silence of the kind you never forget. It was as if the city had suffered a nuclear cataclysm that had spared only the buildings. Houses, flats, office blocks, schools and hotels stood empty and open, as they had been vacated four years earlier when the Khmer Rouge marched the occupants into the countryside, many to their death. Personal possessions lay trampled on a front path, a tricycle crushed and rusted in the gutter, a pair of glasses on an open page. There was little electricity and no water safe to drink; bodies were still being found in wells. At the railway station, trains stood empty at various stages of interrupted departure. Pieces of burned clothing fluttered on the platform. As they abandoned Phnom Penh, the Khmer Rouge had set fire to a carriage filled with wounded civilians.

Beside the abandoned airport was a pyramid of rusting

cars, piled on top of each other. Some of them had been new when their owners were forced to throw away the ignition keys and push them on to the pile, which also included ambulances, a fire engine, refrigerators, washing machines, hairdryers, generators, television sets, telephones and typewriters. It was as if a huge Luddite broom had swept them there at the beginning of 'Year Zero'. The surreal dominated. When the afternoon monsoon broke, the gutters of the city were suddenly awash with money. The streets ran with money, much of it new and unused banknotes, flowing out of the ruined Bank of Cambodia.

In our first hours there, neither Eric nor Gerry took a single frame. Such was our incredulity, or shock. We had no sense of people, of even the remnants of a population; the few human shapes we glimpsed seemed incoherent images, detached from the city itself. Only when we pursued several and watched them forage, did we realise they were children. In a crumbling Esso petrol station an old woman and three emaciated infants squatted around a pot containing a mixture of roots and leaves, which bubbled over a fire fuelled with paper money, hundreds of snapping, crackling brand new notes. Eric's pictures of this morbid irony followed an assignment two months earlier, when he and I had followed Pope John Paul on his return to Poland, and had seen Auschwitz for the first time. Now, we saw it again in South East Asia: a scaled-down version called Tuol Sleng, where a Khmer Rouge gestapo, 'S 21', had systematically murdered thousands. People were mutilated on iron beds and we found their blood and tufts of their hair still on the floor. Eric's picture of one of the beds still chills me. We found eight survivors, including four

children and a one-month old baby. *The Daily Mirror* subsequently devoted thirteen pages to Cambodia over two days, illustrated by Eric's historic photographs. Both issues sold out: itself a response to those who say people will read only pap and the parochial.

We returned to Phnom Penh the following year to find that life had returned, although beneath the surface, there were new dangers; the Khmer Rouge had regrouped on the border with Thailand. Crossing from the Thai side, we entered a Khmer Rouge operations base and met the commander, who was known to the foreign aid relief workers as 'Pol Pot's Himmler'. He told us his name was Nam Phan, which was probably a military alias. Although he was middle-aged, he had an unusually youthful face; Eric's strange portrait is of a smiling teenager with very old and static eyes. The following year, we were planning another trip to Cambodia when Eric fell seriously ill and died. My life changed as never before, as it did following the death of David Munro.

These pages are dedicated to Eric's memory, and to the memory of David Munro, who died in 1999. David and I made many documentary films together: in Cambodia, Vietnam, East Timor, Burma, the Philippines, Mexico and the United States. There is an opening sequence in our first film *Do You Remember Vietnam* (1978) of children playing in a street in Saigon. They bob and weave and run in circles in the monsoon rain, their arms outstretched like the wings of attacking aircraft. A little girl, a peanut seller, runs with them, feigning terror. David had watched the children from a distance, waiting for the light to turn, then he directed the camera in such a way that their play in the film is both a *danse macabre* and an expression of human vulnerability against the savagery of great power. Without violence or bloodshed, it is one of the most telling images of war ever shown.

As a film director, David had an acute understanding and use of imagery. You see it in the Cambodian children joyfully splashing in the sunlight through bright yellow fields of mustard flower: a sequence about landmines and which ends with an explosion. You also see it in David's stills photography. I have included here one of his pictures from the Philippines in 1991. Sadly, like Curt Gunther's, his other pictures from this assignment are lost. For me even the one surviving image reflects the grace of David's personality. We had filmed on Smokey Mountain, a massive rubbish dump that rises out of Manila Bay; our old friends Noel Smart and Mel Marr were the crew, and our clothes and shoes seemed to rot on our skin. David's pictures captured the moments of sheer survival of those who lived there: silhouettes drifting through the smoke and haze and ash and acid rain. They are like portraits from Hogarth's London.

Our film was about the unrepayable debt owed by the Philippines to the World Bank, most of it incurred by the dictator Marcos, who stole billions of dollars. Repaying just the interest consumes most of the Philippines' budget, while the poor, who are the majority of Filipinos, are denied proper health care, housing and education. We filmed Eddie, his wife Teresita and their four children, who lived in the barrio at the foot of Smokey Mountain. Eddie was a fisherman on one of the southern islands until cash cropping, most of it prawns for restaurant tables in America and Europe, forced him to find a life in Manila. From scavenging and collecting pieces of glass, tin and plastic, he made less than two dollars a day: just enough to supply his family with their next meal. He and the thousands on Smokey Mountain are the face workers of a modern poverty reinforced by debt, their lives a metaphor for the majority of humanity we in the West rarely glimpse. David's almost ghostly photographs, of which, alas, we could find the negatives of only one, tell their truth.

I wish to express my appreciation to the Barbican for taking up the idea of the exhibition with such enthusiasm and flair. I thank warmly John Hoole, Carol Brown, Conrad Bodman, Sophie Persson and Alison Green; and Miranda Glover and Joe Ewart. I am grateful to Peter Cook and John Churchill of *The Mirror*'s picture archives for a Herculean job of finding photographs we believed were lost. These include the work of Shigeru Oda, with whom I worked in Hiroshima in 1967 and whose pictures of ailing and poverty-stricken survivors of the atomic bombing are a rare record of Japan's forgotten outcasts. I thank John Garrett for his invaluable support in getting the exhibition started and for his fine printing of Eric Piper's and my pictures; and to all the photographers, including Chris Menges, Peter Stone, Anastasia Vrachnos, Keith Bernstein and John Giannini. If this show and book offer inspiration to a new generation of eyewitness photographers, encouraging them and newspaper and magazine readers to demand a renewal of their craft, it will have been worthwhile.

John Pilger, June 2001

DAILY Mirror

Wednesday, September 12, 1979   8p

WORLD EXCLUSIVE

Report by
JOHN PILGER

Pictures by
ERIC PIPER

Death of a Nation

The £11 million ransom mistake

TYCOON Rolf Schild denied last night that kidnappers holding his wife and daughter were demanding £11 million.

He hinted that the ransom was nearer £1 million.

Mr. Schild dropped his multi-million pound bombshell in a television interview.

The London businessman was speaking for the first time since he was released by Sardinian bandits last week to raise the ransom for his wife Daphne, 51, and daughter Annabel, 15.

During the BBC news interview, he said: "The demand is not £11

It may be £1m says tycoon

million. It is nearer the amount mentioned in the papers as being average for this type of kidnap in Sardinia.

That would put the ransom at around £1 million.

Mr. Schild, 55, did not explain why the £11 million figure emerged. It was first reported by Reuters agency in Sardinia but last night

— Turn to Page Two

SCHILD: A TV bombshell

AN INCREDIBLE human disaster has happened in Cambodia, a once peaceful and gentle land in South East Asia. Perhaps more than two million people—a third of the population—have been killed by a fanatical regime whose apparent aim was to wipe out anyone and anything connected with the modern world and to return a whole nation to "Year Zero": the dawn of an age of slavery, without families and sentiment, without machines, schools, books, medicine, music.

The evidence of murder is plentiful. Like the cracked skulls, above, which were dug out from mass graves near Angkor Wat by villagers who had lost relatives.

For four years there has been almost no-contact with people inside Cambodia; its borders were sealed. JOHN PILGER, in Cambodia, sends the first of two world exclusive reports.

PLEASE TURN TO PAGE 3

The Daily Mirror devoted most of one issue to a world exclusive report from Cambodia by me and photographer Eric Piper. It was one of the few *Mirrors* ever to sell out and was followed by an ITV documentary, *Year Zero: The Silent Death of Cambodia*, which I made with David Munro. An unprecedented response from readers and viewers paid for the first humanitarian relief flights from the West since the fall of Pol Pot.

Cover of The Daily Mirror, 12 September, 1979

When I arrived in Cambodia with Eric Piper we were met by many surreal sights. During the monsoon rain, the streets of Phnom Penh ran, literally, with money. Unused banknotes flowed from the ruined national bank, blown up by the Khmer Rouge as they retreated. Starving children tried to light fires with them, beneath pots of roots and leaves.

ERIC PIPER, 1979

When the Khmer Rouge marched into Phnom Penh on 17 April, 1975, they brought a grim sense of theatre. Owners of private cars were forced to throw away their ignition keys and push their cars on to a pile, which also included ambulances, washing machines, television sets, typewriters. When we arrived, it looked as if a huge Luddite broom had swept them there. Along with pyramids of skulls, it was one of many monuments to Year Zero, 'the beginning of the end of the age of machines'.

ERIC PIPER, 1979

Nam Phan, a senior Khmer Rouge commander, at his base just across the Thai border. Known as 'The Butcher' and 'Pol Pot's Himmler', he was given humanitarian supplies by Western aid agencies at the urging of the United States, which in the 1980s saw the restoration of the Khmer Rouge as a means of bringing pressure on its recently victorious enemy, Vietnam.

Eric Piper, 1980

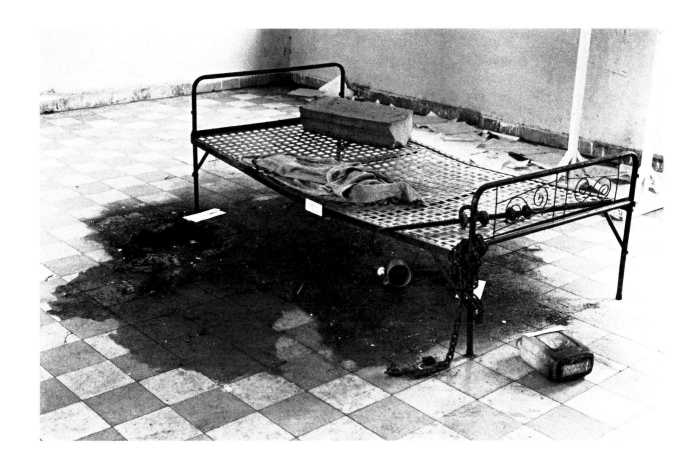

The Khmer Rouge Gestapo, known as 'S21', tortured to death more than 20,000 men, women and children at Tuol Sleng, a former school in Phnom Penh. People were mutilated on iron beds like this one, which was still surrounded by blood and tufts of hair when we found it.

The sign at a site near Phnom Penh, where victims of Tuol Sleng torture centre were buried. The English translation reads, 'Mass grave of more than 100 victims children and women whose majority were naked.'

JOHN PILGER, 1989

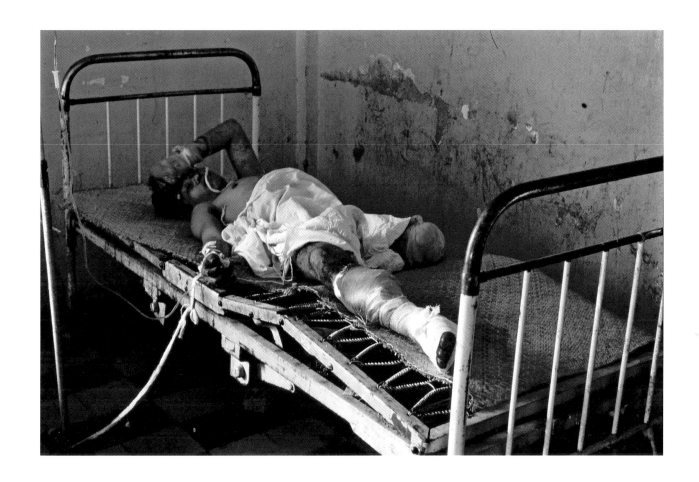

Hearn Boung, a young man who stepped on a land mine, lies in Battambang Hospital in western Cambodia. The hospital lacked almost everything, including blood. He died soon afterwards.

NIC DUNLOP, 1991

The democratically elected leader of Burma, Aung San Suu Kyi, has endured house arrest and harassment by the military dictatorship since her party, the National League for Democracy, won an overwhelming victory in 1990. The generals, who had never expected to lose the election that followed a popular uprising, arrested more than 200 members of the new parliament and gave them prison sentences of up to 25 years. In this photograph, although under threat and constant surveillance, Aung San Suu Kyi and other leading members of the NLD meet at her home.

Nic Dunlop, 1996

A Burmese boy scavenges for bricks after his family was forcibly 'relocated' to a desolate site near Mandalay. The military regime has a policy of dispersing long-established communities and ethnic groups to where their 'voluntary labour' can best be exploited.

Nic Dunlop, 1996

In Burma, which is distinguished by probably the worst human rights record on earth, the Western tobacco companies are major investors.

NIC DUNLOP, 1996

Children work on a road near Pegu in central Burma. Bonded labour and child labour are used extensively on infrastructure projects. In a crash-programme to restore the neglected infrastructure – roads, bridges, airports, railways – the regime has turned Burma into a vast slave labour camp. The generals claim many of the workers are 'convicted criminals'. This term can embrace a person guilty of winning an election or speaking publicly about democracy (five years' hard labour), or of singing a political song (seven years' hard labour).

Nic Dunlop, 1996

Desi is a worker in an 'economic processing zone' near Jakarta, where famous brands of clothes and shoes are made for sale in the West. She holds a pair of boxer shorts that are sold in high street shops in Britain for £8 a pair. She earns 83 pence for working up to twelve hours a day. This is half the amount calculated by the Indonesian government as a living wage.

ANASTASIA VRACHNOS, 2000

In the mid-1960s, more than a million people were killed and thousands imprisoned when General Suharto seized power in Indonesia. Heru Atmotjo was a young airforce officer who supported the deposed independence leader, Sukarno. He spent fifteen years in solitary confinement, and like many 'tapols' – political prisoners – his spirit did not break. Here, he proudly wears the Star of Indonesia, presented to him by President Sukarno and which his wife had kept hidden during his years of imprisonment.

ANASTASIA VRACHNOS, 2000

Indonesia 33

Madame Thai Thi Tinh, with the decorations and photographs of her husband and sons, whose sacrifices symbolised the Vietnamese nation. Her husband was killed at the battle of Dien Bien Phu, which, in 1954, saw the French finally defeated in Vietnam. Her three sons died fighting the Americans more than twenty years later.

DAVID MUNRO, 1995

American officers in their air-conditioned headquarters in Saigon, with a computer that 'proved' they were winning the war. A reliance on machines, and unreality, characterised the American presence in Vietnam.

PHILIP JONES GRIFFITHS, 1970

A GI in a Saigon crowd (centre) has his pocket artfully picked.

PHILIP JONES GRIFFITHS, 1970

Poverty and families divided by the war thrust Vietnamese girls into prostitution from as young as twelve. Drugs came with the American invasion; and after the war, a quarter of a million prostitutes were treated for addiction. It could be said that the paid-for rape in this photograph symbolises the rape of Vietnam.

Philip Jones Griffiths, 1970

In January, 1968, the National Liberation Front, known by the Americans as the Vietcong, attacked South Vietnam's cities in the 'Tet Offensive'. They fought their way into the great American military bases and the US embassy in Saigon; and for the first time the American public was left in little doubt that the war was lost. Yet, under Presidents Nixon and Ford, the war continued for another seven years, with more Vietnamese killed than during all of the preceding years. Here, a soldier of the Washington-based Saigon regime kneels over a civilian seriously wounded in one of the many Tet battles.

PHILIP JONES GRIFFITHS, 1968

A captured soldier of the National Liberation Front. Unlike GIs and the American-trained army of the regime in Saigon, the NLF or 'VC' were lightly armed and carried few personal supplies. Their transport was mostly on foot or by bicycle. They were southerners, a fact at odds with Washington's claim that South Vietnam was invaded by North Vietnam.

Philip Jones Griffiths, 1970

A boy forages for anything of value on Smokey
Mountain, a massive pile of rubbish near Manila.
More than 5,000 people eke out a living amidst
the acrid smoke and stench. The majority of
Filipinos live in abject poverty, while most of the
national budget goes on repaying interest on
international debts incurred, mostly, by the former
dictatorship of Ferdinand Marcos.

DAVID MUNRO, 1991

The occupation of East Timor by the Indonesian military dictatorship of General Suharto lasted for more than twenty-three years, supported indirectly by Western governments and largely ignored by the Western media. More than 200,000 East Timorese, a third of the population, died as a direct result. Proportionally, this was a greater carnage than that instigated by Pol Pot in Cambodia. With almost no help reaching them from the outside world, the ingenuity and bravery of the resistance was remarkable. For secretly making resistance posters, this youth risks arrest, torture and death.

STEVE COX, 1991

Forced to line up with the police, two elderly East Timorese women add to the façade of a peaceful, Indonesian-ruled island. They are watching a show of Timorese dance and culture put on by the occupiers for a group of international observers. Those refusing to take part were arrested.

East Timorese boys among rocks turned white by Agent Orange, a defoliant first used in Vietnam, and sprayed from the air by Indonesian pilots in aircraft supplied by the United States. The aircraft operated in the central mountain range, where tens of thousands of people had fled the invasion. Agent Orange contains dioxin, one of the deadliest-known poisons, which remains in the soil and water, and is the cause of miscarriages and birth deformities.

Steve Cox, 1991

An East Timorese boy watches Indonesian troops pass through the streets of Dili. These demonstrations by the occupiers were frequent and meant to intimidate.

Snatched from his hand, a traditional military sword belonging to an old Timorese man is inspected by an Indonesian soldier. The anxious faces reflect the family's fear – a fear that was like a presence in occupied East Timor.

Steve Cox, 1991

Bangladesh is one of the world's poorest countries. With most of its landmass lying below sea level, the population is vulnerable to the great storms and tidal waves that sweep up the Bay of Bengal. Thousands die in these almost routine calamities, which could be prevented by a comprehensive network of dykes. Some dykes have been built, but resources are scarce. More than any country, Bangladesh will suffer the effects of global warming, as the seas rise. This was a camp of flood victims in Dacca, the capital. Many are desperately hungry.

ERIC PIPER, 1974

In Bangladesh, great floods bring starvation. Children are usually the first to die.

ERIC PIPER, 1974

In 1971, East Pakistan became Bangladesh after a war of independence that gave Bengalis their first national homeland. At a victory rally in the stadium in Dacca, the capital, five young men accused of collaborating with the Pakistanis were brought before the crowd. Western photographers, who had covered the war, were present, and several sensed they might also be playing a part. This photograph is the first of a series of four that tells a disturbing story.

PENNY TWEEDIE, 1971   **Bangladesh** 49

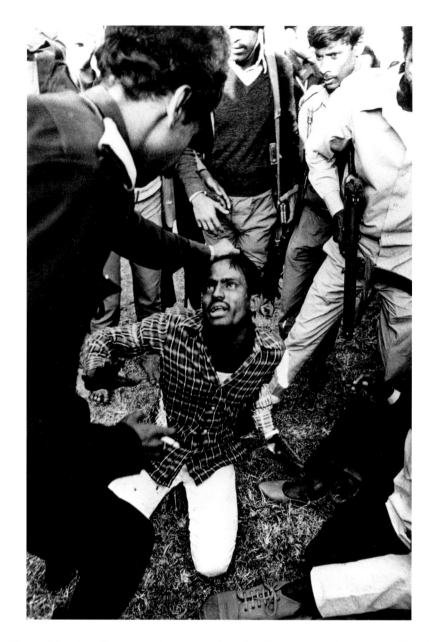

As the 'collaborators' begged for their lives, it was becoming clear that the event was being staged largely for the benefit of the photographers. Penny Tweedie was one who decided to leave, hoping this would stop the gruesome show.

PENNY TWEEDIE, 1971

This was the last photograph Penny Tweedie took before she and two other journalists pointedly walked out of the stadium.

When they returned, they found the young men had been executed by bayoneting. The complete series of photographs, with the actual killings, won an American Pulitzer Prize for one of the photographers who stayed. Other photographers, who were not present, were critical of those who walked away. The moral dilemma and professional responsibilities of this episode are still debated by those who cover war and other civil upheaval.

PENNY TWEEDIE, 1971

On 21 March, 1965, one of the momentous marches of the American civil rights movement set out from Selma, Alabama. Five days later, more than 25,000 people entered the state capital, Montgomery. Led by Martin Luther King, the Selma march helped bring about the enactment, six months later, of a Voting Rights Bill, which enfranchised many black Americans who had been denied the vote.

MATT HERRON, 1965

A Mississippi cop wrests an American flag from a small black boy, having already confiscated his 'no more police brutality' placard.

Matt Herron, 1965

In the 1960s, America's ghettos erupted in protest against the appalling living conditions of most black people. Wilma Ferguson, aged 70, lived in two rooms in a condemned tenement building in New York's Harlem. Water from broken pipes streamed down the walls, the electric power came and went, along with rats, cockroaches and burglars. Transport and other public services were intermittent or non-existent. From her doorstep, she could see the Empire State Building.

KEN REGAN, 1968

An unemployed man and his two children in the kitchen of their slum in Harlem, New York.

KEN REGAN, 1968

A resident of Bogalusa, Louisiana, commenting on a passing civil rights march.

MATT HERRON, 1965

Waiting for the dole in Detroit, 1976, where seventy per cent of the work force was officially jobless. Today, Americans who can find intermittent or 'flexible' work are not registered as unemployed: in this way, millions of jobless have 'disappeared'. With declining wages and benefits, many Americans have to hold two or three 'flexible' jobs to maintain the standard of living of the 1970s.

KEN REGAN, 1976

In the 1970s, the 41st Precinct of the New York Police Department in the Bronx was the most violent and impoverished in the United States. Known as Fort Apache, the bunkered police station had a 'Do Not Cross' barrier *inside* the station. A sign over the door read, 'Superior officers bulletin: assume that all combatants use high power military-type weapons for sniping, and Molotov cocktails for ambushing.'

Ken Regan, 1971

A member of the New York 'Guardian Angels'. His street name is Finger. In the 1980s, the Angels were 600 allegedly unarmed volunteers patrolling New York's subway system, protecting commuters from muggers. For a time, they enjoyed widespread public approval. 'We are not vigilantes,' said Finger. 'We are of the citizenry'.

Ken Regan, 1981

Joe Colombo, the leading New York Mafia boss, in 1971. A novel and a movie, *The Godfather*, starring Marlon Brando, were based on his life, which ended soon after this photograph was taken. He was gunned down in the street by a rival mob. 'Mr Pilger', he said, 'you need anything, or anyone's bothering you, you just call this number.'

President Richard Nixon with his wife, Pat, daughters and son-in-law, following his narrow election victory over Hubert Humphrey in 1968. Nixon's paranoia led to him authorising the infamous burglary of the Democratic Party's national headquarters at the Watergate building in 1972. The bleak irony, for him, was that his black deeds were unnecessary. In November of that year, he was re-elected by an historic margin, winning all but one state. He was forced to resign in disgrace in 1974.

KEN REGAN, 1968

President Jimmy Carter following his election victory in 1976. A devout Christian with a famous smile, Carter projected himself as Mr Clean in the wake of the Watergate scandals. 'I shall never lie', he said. He also said, 'Human rights will be first and foremost in American foreign policy'. Two striking examples of Carter's foreign policy were Nicaragua and East Timor. He supported the Somoza dictatorship in Nicaragua, pressuring the International Monetary Fund to hand over $25 million without conditions, weeks before Somoza was overthrown. Somoza stole the lot. In East Timor, without Carter's backing, the Indonesian invaders may well have been beaten back. Instead, during 1977-79, the genocide reached its height, thanks principally to a constant supply of American intelligence and weapons to General Suharto's forces. An estimated quarter of the East Timorese population perished during this period.

KEN REGAN, 1976

In 1976, when he was considering running for president, Edward Kennedy went south to 'pay respects' to George Wallace, the infamous governor of Alabama. Kennedy believed Wallace might help the surviving brother of John and Robert, 'deliver the South' for him. 'Y'know,' said Wallace, 'between us conservatives and them liberals there's always some common ground.'

KEN REGAN, 1976

I interviewed Robert Kennedy as he flew into Los Angeles for polling day in the California primary election on 4 June, 1968. Beside him sat his wife, Ethel. When he had set out on the road to the White House earlier that year, Kennedy supported the Vietnam war and his 'liberal' record on civil rights was mixed. By the summer, he opposed the war and promised a 'new dawn' to America's minorities.

He told me, 'Maybe I can never suffer like the blacks, the Indians, and the Chicanos do. But, Jesus Christ, I'm the one to stand up for them'.

'Why?' I asked.

'I can be President of the United States.'

'So can Hubert Humphrey or Richard Nixon.'

'They can't be President *Kennedy*.'

The famous rabbit smile enveloped his face. He was shot the next day.

CURT GUNTHER, 1968

Daily Mirror

5d. Thursday, June 6, 1968   No. 20,945

LOS ANGELES, WEDNESDAY, 12.15 a m

Robert Kennedy lies stricken by a gunman's bullets—and one of his supporters cries out in disbelief..

GOD! NOT AGAIN!

SENATOR Bobby Kennedy lies sprawled on a hotel floor. As arms reach out to comfort him, his eyes mirror disbelief and a terrible sense of helplessness. Seconds before, a gunman's bullets struck Bobby down in his moment of political triumph in the California Primary poll. Now, still conscious, he stays motionless amid

the incredible pandemonium which has erupted around him. "God! Not again!" cried a friend as he saw Bobby lying there—shot like his brother John before him. The time in Los Angeles was 12.15 a.m. The place: the kitchen of the Ambassador Hotel. And the date America will remember with shame: Wednesday, June 5, 1968. Just four and a half years after Dallas.

JOHN PILGER, the Mirror's Journalist of the Year, and George Gale, the Mirror's columnist, were in the hotel where Kennedy was shot. Pilger reports on Page 2. Gale's report is on the Centre Pages.

More on Kennedy on the Back Page and Page 11.

On 5 June, 1968, Robert Kennedy was shot as he left the ballroom of the Ambassador Hotel in Los Angeles. He had just acknowledged victory in the California primary election, which almost certainly assured his nomination as the Democratic Party's candidate in the presidential election in November. He would then have faced Richard Nixon, whom most observers believed he would beat to the White House. I was standing next to Kennedy when the assassin, Sirhan Sirhan, fired a volley of bullets, Kennedy died the next day.

Cover of The Daily Mirror, 6 June, 1968

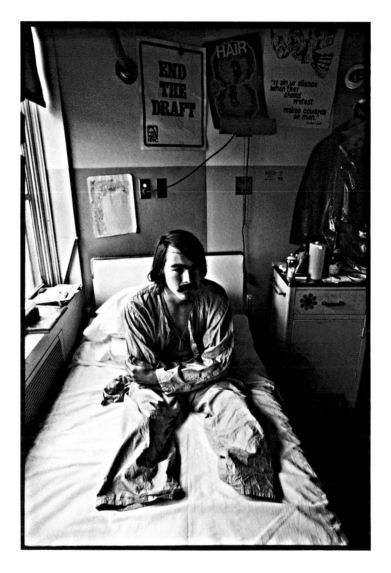

A veteran of the Vietnam war in a military hospital in New York, in 1978. He was twenty when he stepped on a mine, losing both legs. (I regret that his name has been lost.) Contrary to myth, and unlike World War Two, eighty per cent of young Americans who fought in Vietnam were volunteers. They were mostly from the working class; they had no student deferments, which enabled many middle-class young men to evade the draft. On their return, there were no parades; they were shunned. In 1979, a Harris opinion poll found that the majority of Americans believed the Vietnam veterans 'were made suckers of, having to risk their lives in the wrong war at the wrong time.'

KEN REGAN, 1978

Michael Schwarz at home in Bugler, West Virginia, shortly after his release from prison, where he was serving a life sentence for murder. Schwarz was a US Marine who served in Vietnam, one of a five-man patrol that shot dead eleven women and five children in 1969. His orders were to conduct a 'search and destroy' operation in a 'free fire zone' and report a 'body count'. In practice, this meant killing anything that moved. It was only after the revelation of the massacre of hundreds of civilians in the village of My Lai in 1968 that the US military began prosecuting soldiers for 'isolated atrocities'. The atrocities were neither isolated nor contrary to military policy. More than three million people died in the Vietnam war, most of them civilians; other estimates are higher. Schwarz, a private, and others convicted of similar crimes, were quietly released after serving a fraction of their sentence. No senior officers were ever charged.

KEN REGAN, 1971

Beallsville, a working-class town in Ohio, lost more sons in the Vietnam war, proportionally, than any community in the United States. According to a telegram his parents received from the Pentagon, Rick Rucker, aged nineteen, was killed by a 'friendly rocket while storming a Vietcong bunker'. His father later learned there was no Vietcong bunker, 'just a bunch of guys sitting around a latrine area when some American, somehow, accidentally blew them up. They were havin' a crap. Nothin' more than that.' In 1970, more than half the Americans who died in Vietnam were killed by their own side – 'friendly fire' – or in accidents. Here, Betty and Kenneth Rucker stand outside their home with the decorations awarded to Rick.

MATT HERRON, 1970

The grave of Jack Pittman overlooking Beallsville High School, where he was captain of the football and basketball teams. His mother, Maegene Pittman, had never heard of Vietnam when Jack was called up at the age of nineteen. 'I thought it was somewhere near Panama,' she said, 'real close and threatening.'

MATT HERRON, 1970

Mike Sulsona at home in Brooklyn, New York. He was nineteen when a landmine in Vietnam made him a double amputee and destroyed his hearing. 'I gave my Bronze Star to the kid next door,' he said. 'He likes to play soldiers with it.'

KEN REGAN, 1978

Workers leaving a May Day meeting in Johannesburg find riot police blocking their way. The Congress of South African Trade Unions had called a national strike in which a million and a half workers took part. It was one of many dramatic events organised by the black trade unions that helped bring down the apartheid regime.

PAUL WEINBERG, 1985

A lone woman protests as South African soldiers occupying her township, Soweto, roll by in armoured military vehicles, known as 'hippos'.

Edith Ventner, a Johannesburg socialite, at her couturier's. Like many South African whites, she says she never supported apartheid. The necklace she is wearing is worth £100,000. In the 'new' South Africa, the white five per cent of the population still control more than eighty per cent of the nation's wealth.

Keith Bernstein, 1997

The living conditions of landless farmers and their families in South Africa's Eastern Cape in 1997. Following the end of apartheid, more than eighty per cent of prime agricultural land remains in the hands of whites, whose property rights are guaranteed under the constitution approved by the African National Congress.

KEITH BERNSTEIN, 1997

A street fighter of Nicaragua's Sandinistas, the popular revolutionary movement that overthrew the dictator Anastasio Somoza in 1979. The Somoza family had ruled Nicaragua since 1933, when the US marines handed them the country, following a twenty-one year occupation and unsuccessful war against a guerrilla army led by Cesar Augusto Sandino, a national hero. Sandino was subsequently murdered by Somoza, whose long, repressive rule was guaranteed by the United States. President Nixon said, 'He may be a son-of-a-bitch, but he's our son-of-a-bitch'. When they came to power, the Sandinistas instigated land reform borrowed from the Co-operative Movement in England, an adult literacy programme, universal education and healthcare. These have since been reversed, following the successful 'contra' war, planned and funded by the Central Intelligence Agency.

Susan Meiselas, 1979

In the final stages of their revolution in 1979, the Sandinistas often used symbolism as a weapon. Here, a portrait of dictator Somoza is burned with the body of one of his feared National Guardsmen. Somoza ran Nicaragua like a family business. His family owned almost half the arable land, controlling the coffee, sugar and beef industries. He owned the national airline. If you bought a foreign car, you bought it from a Somoza company. He owned all the cement and brick factories, even Managua's sewers, right up to the manhole covers. A calypso popular in the 1940s began: 'A guy asked the dictator if he had any farms. The dictator said he had only one. It was Nicaragua.'

SUSAN MEISELAS, 1979

Two children rescued from a house destroyed by a 1000-pound bomb dropped by the Nicaraguan dictator Somoza on his own people during the Sandinista uprising. They died soon afterwards.

SUSAN MEISELAS, 1979

It is traditional that the Pope prays for the leadership of every country he visits. In 1983, he prayed for the murderous tyranny of El Salvador. Flying on to Nicaragua, he refused to pray for the Sandinista government which had the support of the majority of its people. Here, before a crowd in Managua, he is chastising priests who were also Sandinistas. That he was overshadowed by huge images of Sandino and the Sandinista president, Daniel Ortega, was an irony not lost on his audience.

SUSAN MEISELAS, 1983 **Nicaragua** 79

Chanchalgar Gosi, who once owned a shop in Nairobi, uses the pavement to write desperate letters to the British High Commission. Caught between a local campaign to Africanise commercial life (inspired by the notorious Idi Amin) and a resistance by the British government to granting them entry, thousands of East African Asians found themselves stateless, even though most had British citizenship.

Marion Kaplan, 1968

A destitute East African Asian, who cannot work in Kenya and cannot go to Britain, waits for help in the Social Service League, a Nairobi charity that dispensed food and medicine.

MARION KAPLAN, 1968

Nairobi railway station in August, 1972. A train passes through from Idi Amin's Uganda, with some of the 50,000 Asians given ninety days to leave the country. The Conservative government of Edward Heath granted them asylum.

MARION KAPLAN, 1972

Poverty in Japan is often subtle. This was not true in Hiroshima in 1967. Many of the 70,000 survivors of the atomic bomb lived in extreme poverty in slums beside the river. They were outcasts, victims of superstition, ignorance and rumour. It was believed that if a survivor so much as sneezed, those nearby would contract radiation sickness. People lied about the past in order to marry, get a job and enrol their children in schools. Many left Hiroshima and began new lives under assumed names.

SHIGERU ODA, 1967

In Hiroshima, where the atomic bomb fell on 6 August, 1945, the people who did not die immediately have suffered ever since, many dying slowly from a range of cancers. This man, attended by his wife, died soon after the photograph was taken in 1967. He remembered the hours after the explosion. 'Everything was still and quiet,' he said. 'There were young girls naked, not saying anything. Some of them had no skin or hair. I thought I was dead.'

SHIGERU ODA, 1967

A landmark event for the Aboriginal struggle was the 1982 Commonwealth Games in Brisbane. Protestors were able to draw international attention to the extreme deprivation suffered by the first Australians, who had few of the human rights won by indigenous peoples in other colonial countries. Today, black infant mortality is three times that of white children, life expectancy is among the lowest in the world, and rates of suicides among the young, and imprisonment, are the highest in the world.

PENNY TWEEDIE, 1982

Australia's hidden history is Aboriginal. In 1992, the High Court recognised native title, ending the historical fiction that Australia was an 'empty land' when the British landed at Botany Bay in the eighteenth century. However, in 1998, the federal government countered this with legislation that effectively took away the common law rights that the court said belonged to the Aborigines. Nothing as openly racist has been enacted in a modern, democratic parliament. The United Nations has since distinguished Australia with its first adverse finding on racial discrimination against a western nation.

PENNY TWEEDIE, 1982

David Malaugi and his family in 1978. David was a celebrated artist whose painting appeared on the Australian one-dollar note. Like many Aboriginal artists, whose work is shown all over the world, he received little of the material benefits. He and his family, standing in front of their shack, epitomise the dignity, hurt and enduring poverty of the Aboriginal people. He died in 1998.

White and black Australia, Alice Springs.

GERRIT FOKKEMA, 1987

By the 1960s, Australians could boast the most equitable spread of personal income in the world. Twenty years later, this had been lost in the most spectacular redistribution of wealth since the Second World War, instigated by the Labor government of Bob Hawke and his treasurer, Paul Keating. De-regulation and privatisation spawned a new 'bonanza class', their fortunes built on easy borrowing, property deals, tax avoidance and laws often tailored for them. A new, entrenched poverty appeared, as the gulf widened. By 1987, almost a fifth of Australia's children were born poor. Trailer parks, like this one in the west of Sydney, where the impoverished young and old lived, became an extension of suburbia.

GERRIT FOKKEMA, 1987

A pensioner in the garden of his trailer home in western Sydney.

GERRIT FOKKEMA, 1987

In the 1950s, the British Government used central Australia as an atomic test site. Patrick Connolly, who served with the Royal Air Force at the Maralinga test site, was threatened with prosecution after he revealed that the Aboriginal population was given no warning of the tests. 'During the two and a half years I was there,' he said, 'I would have seen 400-500 Aborigines in contaminated areas. We just shooed them off like rabbits.' This lavatory was one of a number of household structures built to test their resistance to a nuclear blast. Appropriately, it is all that remains of the Maralinga site.

GERRIT FOKKEMA, 1987

During the 1860s, one in nine of the male population of Australia was Chinese. These were miners and merchants who came for the gold rush. Most intended to return home, but many died on the goldfields, as paupers. The Chinese were subjected to a racist brutality similar to that suffered by the Aboriginal population. In the 1980s, Denis O'Hoy, here beneath pictures of his grandparents, was a tram driver and local historian in the gold rush town of Bendigo, Victoria.

GERRIT FOKKEMA, 1987

Brian Day and Barry Wright, much decorated Australian veterans of the Vietnam war. Both suffered serious illnesses associated with the effects of dioxin, the poison in the herbicide spray, 'Agent Orange', which the Americans used to destroy almost half of Vietnam's forests. Brian Day was in charge of a 'black team' that carried out enemy assassinations for the US command. An American officer told him: 'We like having you guys here ... it's like the British having Gurkhas, we have the Australians.'

GERRIT FOKKEMA, 1987

Volunteers of the remarkable Green Cross in El Salvador during the civil war of the 1980s. Most were teenagers, as young as fifteen. Founded in France during World War Two, 'to give human warmth as well as first aid', the Green Cross went into the most dangerous parts of El Salvador, where the Red Cross refused to go. Many were injured and 'disappeared'.

Eric Piper, 1981

A photo album of victims of the 'security forces' of El Salvador, compiled by human rights workers. Between 1980 and 1986, tens of thousands of people were murdered by military special forces, in various guises, trained and funded by the United States. President Reagan himself 'certified' that the vicious El Salvador regime satisfied the 'human rights criteria' required by Congress for American arms shipments to continue.

ERIC PIPER, 1981

Enoch Powell supporters listening to their hero in Wolverhampton.

JOHN GARRETT, 1970

In the late 1960s, the Tory politician Enoch Powell could claim to have set the political agenda on race relations in Britain with his apocalyptic 'warnings' of the consequences of a multi-racial society. In spite of his racism, he was lionised by sections of the intelligentsia as a significant thinker and orator. This said less about Powell and rather more about the veiled racism in the British establishment.

JOHN GARRETT, 1970

Until 1972, British miners were among the lowest paid primary industrial workers in the Western world. Two years later, the miners struck for a minimum wage of £35 a week, £45 for coal-face workers. During January, 1974, I spent several shifts in a deep seam colliery in Murton, County Durham. Joe Cardy, pictured here leaving the pithead at the end of a night shift, was a big man who worked in a tunnel three and a half feet high and slightly wider than his shoulders. The roof rained a constant drizzle of white slush. For this, he received a 'wet rate' of eleven pence a shift. Like many miners who suffered a range of illnesses and injuries, Joe died several years later, literally worked to death. At the end of the Great Strike of 1984-5, Murton Colliery was one of the last pits to accept defeat. Although profitable and with abundant coal stocks, it was closed by the Conservative government in 1991.

Tom Buist, 1974

Women Against Pit Closures demonstrate at Easington colliery in County Durham in 1991, the year before Michael Heseltine closed it, along with most of the remaining mines that had survived the aftermath of the Great Strike. A spontaneous eruption of public support for the miners, and a High Court ruling that Heseltine had acted illegally, did not stop 10,000 men from losing their jobs, and eventually the unnecessary demise of a great industry.

JOHN GARRETT, 1991   **United Kingdom** 99

Unemployed Durham miners outside a labour exchange.

JOHN GARRETT, 1994

An impoverished Liverpool family in 1976. A quarter of a century later, one British child in four grows up in poverty.

At the height of the British Empire, Liverpool, the leading seaport of the world's greatest maritime nation, had worse poverty and generated greater profit than anywhere in Britain. Today, the profit has moved elsewhere, and the poverty remains. With one of Europe's highest number of homeless people and people living in sub-standard dwellings, the city has streets of empty, derelict houses. In the general election in 2001, almost two-thirds of voters in one Liverpool constituency did not vote.

John Garrett, 2001

Two police officers examine a man on the ground in Toxteth, a poor and violent area of Liverpool. One of his companions spots photographer, John Garrett. With the police distracted, three of the men get into a car and a high-speed chase ensues. Fortunately, Garrett's car is faster.

A shop in Toxteth, Liverpool, protected by barbed wire.

JOHN GARRETT, 2001

Beyond the 'booming economy'. The Village Inn, Sunderland.

JOHN GARRETT, 2001

A housing estate in Sunderland. On many such estates the windows are boarded up, there is damp and rats and up to seventy per cent unemployment. According to a study for Bristol University, in 2001 more than five million Britons are living in conditions of absolute poverty.

John Garrett, 2001

Selling British missiles at the Farnborough arms fair, 1994. In the 1960s, the motor industry was the biggest single manufacturer in Britain. With the coming of Margaret Thatcher and her political heirs, much of traditional manufacturing has been dismantled, disinvested and sold off. One exception is arms, of which Britain is the world's second-largest exporter, after the United States. No other export sector is as cosseted by governments with secret subsidies and 'soft loans', such as those to the dictatorship in Indonesia, which was supplied with everything lethal from Hawk jets to Rapier missiles. Today, Britain is a major arms supplier to at least five countries with repressive regimes and internal conflict and where the combined death toll runs to almost one million people.

JOHN GARRETT, 1994

Belfast erupts following the shooting of fourteen unarmed marchers by the Parachute Regiment on 30 January, 1972, Bloody Sunday.

JOHN GARRETT, 1972

Another Irish death, another funeral, with the Royal Ulster Constabulary in attendance, as law enforcer or provocateur, depending on which side you were on.

JOHN GARRETT, 1972

Two Russian school teachers, members of the dissident underground in Leningrad in the 1970s. They risked a great deal by speaking to me about the Greek Orthodox priest, Lev Konin, who had been sent to a psychiatric hospital for writing an article critical of the Soviet government's human rights record. We spent a day in various taxis, pretending to be tourists, hoping we were not being followed. On the day Eric Piper and I left for London, someone tried to seize Eric's film. He was unsuccessful. I wrote several times to the teachers, but never received a reply.

ERIC PIPER, 1977

The Russian dissident scientist, Vladimir Slepak, at the door of his besieged apartment in Gorky Street, Moscow, in 1977. Vladimir and his wife, Maria, also a distinguished scientist, had served several terms in prison for 'anti-Soviet activities'. It was clear they were singled out by the authorities because of their work advising the monitory committee of the 1975 Helsinki agreement on human rights, which the Soviet government had signed. 'What is bizarre', said Maria, 'is that those of us who call on the state not to break its own laws are known as dissidents and law-breakers.' Their telephone had been disconnected and their books and letters confiscated. As Eric Piper and I left their apartment, we had to run a gauntlet of a bunch of KGB goons on the stairs. When one of them lunged for Eric's camera, he was seen off by Eric with an inept boot in the shin. The Slepaks endured this kind of intimidation, and much more, every day.

ERIC PIPER, 1977

With thanks to:

Camera 5: Osie Kaynan
Carlton: Nick Lockett and Celia Berry
John Garrett
Steven Gunther
Jacqueline Korn, David Higham Associates
London Features International Ltd
Magnum Photos: Brigitte Lardinois,
Christina Negulescu-Burt and Kim Bourus
Liz Moore
Layhing Sui-Munro
Panos Pictures: Adrian Evans and Michael Regnier
Peter Cook and Syndication International

Picture credits:

Nic Dunlop / Panos Pictures, pp. 27-31
Philip Jones Griffiths / Magnum Photos, pp. 35-39
Curt Gunther / London Features International,
cover and p. 66
Susan Meiselas / Magnum Photos, pp. 76-79
Reuters/Syndication International, pp.66
Syndication International, pp. 47-48 (Eric Piper); 83-84
(Shigeru Oda); 96 (Tom Buist)
Penny Tweedie / Panos Pictures, pp. 49-52
Paul Weinberg / Panos Pictures, pp. 72-73
All others, courtesy the photographers

Photographers' portraits:

Candido N. Alves (Anastasia Vrachnos)
Stewart Attwood (Steve Cox)
Christine DePierro (Philip Jones Griffiths)
Sherran Evans (Penny Tweedie)
Steven Gunther (Curt Gunther)
Graeme Harris (John Garrett)
Maud Larson (Eric Piper)
Eugene Richards (Susan Meiselas)
Jane Hill (David Munro)
John Garrett (John Pilger)
Eric Robins (Marion Kaplan)
Ross Wills (Gerrit Fokkema)

Back cover portrait of John Pilger: John Garrett